C000201105

BOOK PRIZES & AWARDS FOR INDIE AUTHORS

THE ALLI GUIDE TO BEING AN AWARD-WINNING SELF-PUBLISHER

ALLIANCE OF INDEPENDENT AUTHORS

A NOTE ABOUT ALLI

THE ALLIANCE OF INDEPENDENT AUTHORS

This book is one of a number of self-publishing guidebooks and campaign books for authors produced by the Alliance of Independent Authors (ALLi).

If you haven't yet heard of ALLi, it is a global, non-profit association for self-publishing authors. Our mission is ethics and excellence in self-publishing and we bring together thousands of indie authors all over the world who are united behind this mission.

All our profits are reinvested back into the organization for the benefit of our members—and the wider author community.

ALLi is pronounced "ally" (al-eye), and an ally is what we aim to be to self-publishers everywhere. Our name is spelt with a big ALL and small i because our members are like the three musketeers in Dumas's eponymous novel: ALL working for each individual "i", and each for ALL.

ALLi offers members a range of benefits but our real strength is our members, team and advisors, who provide something like the ancient system of craft apprenticeship, with the wisdom of the hive-mind instead of one master.

Our work is fourfold:

- ALLi *advises*, providing best-practice information and education through a <u>Self-Publishing Advice Center</u> that offers a daily blog, weekly livestreams and podcasts, a bookstore of self-publishing guidebooks, and a quarterly member magazine.
- ALLi *monitors* the self-publishing sector through a **watchdog desk**, alerting authors to bad actors and predatory players and running an approved partner program.
- ALLi *campaigns* for the **advancement of indie authors** in the publishing and literary sectors globally (bookstores, libraries, literary events, prizes, grants, awards, and other author organizations), encouraging the provision of publishing and business skills for authors, speaking out against iniquities, and furthering the indie author cause wherever possible.
- ALLi *empowers* independent authors through a wide variety of **member tools and resources** including author forums, contract advice, sample agreements, networking, literary agency representation, and a member care desk.

Headquartered in London, we operate all over the world and at every level, bringing our mission of ethics and excellence in self-publishing to beginner, emerging and experienced authors. Whether you're just starting out, or you're already widely published, ALLi can empower you to make better books, reach more readers, and generate greater profits.

When you join ALLi, you're not just joining an organization, you're becoming part a transformative, self-organising, global author movement. Whether you're self-publishing your first novel or your fiftieth, ALLi is with you every step of the way, with a suite of member benefits that includes free guidebooks, discounts and deals, member forums, contract consultancy, advisory board, literary agency, watchdog and more.

Your membership also supports our advocacy work for indie authors globally, from Alaska to New Zealand and offers access to ALLi's supportive, dynamic community.

If you haven't yet, is it time you joined us?
AllianceIndependentAuthors.org

BOOK AWARD FORMATS
AWARDS CONTESTS AND PRIZES

A re you an indie author who wants to win an award for your writing and publishing? You can.

Indie authors have long been excluded from the most prestigious book prizes, awards, and competitions, but the awards scene is changing. You may be surprised at just how many awards *are* open to you as an indie author. According to Hannah Jacobson, founder of BookAwardPro.com, "Over 92% of all book awards are available to indie and self-published authors," including many that are for indie only.

This guidebook provides the latest updates and steps you need to enter your work in book award programs of all types.

CONTESTS, AWARDS, PRIZES

Traditionally, the words "contest, "award," and "prize" have been used interchangeably when referring to any or all of the book award programs available to authors. In fact there are big distinctions between award formats and types, both in terms of how you take part and the rewards you can expect. For example, as an author you must enter to win a contest or competition but for major literary awards, you must be nominated by a trade publisher, or by yourself as your own publisher.

Before we begin, let's look at the three most popular categories: awards, contests, prizes, so we understand our terms of reference in this guidebook.

What Is a Contest or Competition?

A contest or competition is the easiest to define because you have to "enter" it.

There is an enormous range of competitions in the publishing industry, including contests and competitions for flash fiction, short stories, novellas, and poetry as well as competitions for novels, nonfiction, and memoir. Some contests focus on a specific genre or niche, others are offered on a local basis, or around an institution, such as writing contests for a poem or short story at an opera house or arts center. Check your local libraries or event calendars for possibilities. As with so many things, entering a local contest is a great way to get some recognition while supporting your local literary community. Contests and competitions typically offer cash prizes, scholarships, digital courses, media announcements, publishing services, and more.

What Is a Literary Award?

Literary awards are dedicated to various writing formats or genres, e.g. poetry, novels, or a certain genre of fiction or nonfiction. Some awards are dedicated to works in certain languages, such as the Camões Prize (Portuguese), the Miguel de Cervantes Prize [1] (Spanish, and The Booker Prize[2], the Folio Prize[3], the Pulitzer Prize[4], and the Hugo Awards[5] (English). Other international literary awards include the Jerusalem Prize, the Franz Kafka Prize, and the Nobel Prize.

Most literary awards are structured within one organization (typically a non-profit) as the presenter of the award. Financial and corporate sponsors fund the prize amounts and the award ceremonies.

Literary awards are the most prestigious awards to writers, usually received after a long-term career as an author. You don't "enter" for a literary award, you are nominated, or you are just awarded, as some are conferred without nomination.

Publishers typically nominate their authors. As indie authors, we are our own publishers, so it is up to us to nominate our own books for awards.

What Is a Prize?

A prize is something else again. You receive a prize when you win an award or a contest. The award itself counts as a type of prize because you gain recognition and kudos from having won. But prizes can also include cash, a residency, education, internships, mentorships, a blue ribbon, or something else.

One example of a "prize" without a competition or award is receiving a badge from Amazon for being a #1 New Release or a #1 Bestseller.

Sometimes an award can be all three: a contest, a prize, and an award. This is usually the case with the most prestigious literary awards like the Booker Prize: it is an award, a prize, and a competition. It's also an example of how the three concepts get discussed interchangeably, and confusingly. Such confusion enables myths and misnomers to spread because the lines become blurred.

Today there are numerous literary prizes for books of all genres, themes, and backgrounds, including many that are now open *only* to self-publishers. That's cause for celebration as well as a new opportunity for you to become an award-winning indie author. Many of these awards are prestigious, increasingly high profile, and doing work that we at ALLi wholeheartedly support. Alas, some are the very opposite, and should be approached with caution.

Undoubtedly there will be new awards in both categories in the coming years. This *ALLi Awards and Prizes* guidebook began as a single chapter in our book *Open Up to Indie Authors* and is a core part of that campaign. See **AllianceIndependentAuthors.org/open-up-campaign** for more on that.

While the most prestigious awards like the US National Book

Award, the Booker or the Pulitzer Prize lead the field in bringing honor and prestige as well as sales to a book, awards of all sizes can be leveraged, if you make awards part of your marketing strategy— spreading the word about your book, generating interest among readers and influencers, building fanfare, and making your author sales pages more alluring.

Hannah Jacobson, founder of BookAwardPro.com, points up that one of the reasons why indie authors are not winning awards is that many indies aren't aware they are eligible for some well-known awards such as the Pulitzer Prize, or are too shy to enter. ALLi wants to change that and to encourage indie authors who want to pursue the accolades and increased sales associated with leveraging awards and prizes.

In this guidebook, we examine the major prizes and also the wide-reaching spectrum of contests and awards that are either open to some, open to all, or open specifically to self-published books. We will examine how the contest landscape has changed and what changes have yet to be made. We'll explain how ALLi monitors the awards landscape and rates awards programs. And we'll advise you on how to find the right program for your book and give you tips for entering awards in ways that maximise your chances of a shortlist or a win.

Our aim is to increase the odds for any author who wants to become an award-winning author.

---

1. https://en.wikipedia.org/wiki/Miguel_de_Cervantes_Prize
2. https://en.wikipedia.org/wiki/Booker_Prize
3. https://en.wikipedia.org/wiki/Folio_Prize
4. https://en.wikipedia.org/wiki/Pulitzer_Prize
5. https://en.wikipedia.org/wiki/Hugo_Awards

2

DO BOOK AWARDS MATTER?

An indie author's most important task is production: writing the next book while publishing current and previous books. Entering awards or contests usually costs money and is neither a necessity, nor a sure bet. So do book awards and award contests do what they promise – give you added publicity and help you sell your books?

The short answer is it depends. Firstly, winning a major book award is a clear indicator to the book-buying public of a book's value, at least as perceived by the judges of that prize.

Top literary awards are high profile and make news headlines many times over whenever the winners are announced. Announcements of long lists, short lists, winners, and then the ensuing aftermath all provide valuable publicity opportunities for authors lucky enough to be chosen. This naturally increases awareness, branding, and fame for the book and author.

Top awards also tend to offer substantial cash prizes—$15,000 for the Pulitzer, £50,000 (US$70) for The Booker Prize, and a staggering 8m Swedish Kronor (US$1.2 million) for the Nobel Prize for Literature. Many other benefits may be gained beyond the prize, including increased sales.

A prize sticker—whether as a winner or even a short-listed runner-up—on a book cover has the power to boost sales. Including accolades in book promotions can increase engagement with your ads and sales pages. Promotional service BookBub did A/B tests that showed how including accolades boosted the click-through rate of Featured Deals. Readers responded well to mentions of an author's accolades, including awards and blurbs that named prestigious, genre-specific awards boosted CTRs by up to 25%, with an average increase of 5%.

Award-winning books are also more likely to be picked up for sales of translation and other subsidiary rights, including TV and film, greater visibility for the author's backlist and higher advances in future contracts.

Such benefits can be enjoyed even by the ironic awards, such as the highly regarded Literary Review's infamous Bad Sex in Fiction Award, given to the author who produces the worst description of a sex scene in a novel. Even this kind of award can help to sell more books and raise an author's profile.

With such massive prizes and potential profits for publishers, it is no surprise that the top awards sometimes seem to be little more than a battleground for competing publisher armies. To say that the big trade publishers and their authors are keen to enter is an understatement. Some writers even demand their publisher include an agreement in their contracts to enter their books for major prizes at the publisher's expense.

But indies are different. We are authors who also perform the role of publisher. Thus we can choose whether or not to enter awards. As authors, we might like the ego boost. As publishers, we might decide that we can't afford it, or that it's not priority.

Not all publishers enter their authors into awards, and it's not like you *need* to enter an award in order to sell books. Awards are squarely in the "nice to have" rather than the "must have" bucket. It's completely legitimate to never bother entering an award or contest. Equally, if you do enter or submit, it makes sense to use the award effectively.

"Leveraging an award, from submission to win," is what makes the difference, says BookAwardPro.com founder Hannah Jacobson. "Every award submission should count for something."

Writer Take Care

Just like anything else in the writing and publishing industry, if you're considering submitting your book for a literary award you need to do your homework. If you are awards-inclined, then there's a lot to consider. You need to be able to distinguish between a decent award and one that's a vehicle for profiteering.

The head of ALLi's watchdog desk, John Doppler, assesses contests and awards in a regularly updated list, which includes warnings and recommendations (See Chapter 7, ALLi Watchdog ratings for more on this).

As Jacobson writes, "One award which feels like a 'warning' for one author might feel like a 'perfect fit' for another author." So it's important to find the right award or contest for *your* book.

Book Award Controversies

Great books that were overlooked, lack of diversity and accessibility, "unreadable" highbrow shortlists, judges who picked their spouses' books as the winners—these are just some of the controversies that have bedevilled book awards.

In 2020, Booker Prize judges unable to agree the "best" book of the year divided the prize between two authors. In the 1970s, the same problem was resolved by tossing a coin.

The Booker Prize, formerly known as the Booker Prize for Fiction and the Man Booker Prize, was established in 1969. According to its website, the prize is:

The leading literary award in the English speaking world, which has brought recognition, reward, and readership to outstanding fiction for over 50 years. Awarded annually to the best novel of the year written in English and published in the UK or Ireland. The winner of The Booker Prize receives international publicity which usually leads to a sales boost.

Those words "best novel of the year written in English" go to the heart of a controversy that bedevils the very notion of book awards. The winning book is chosen by an advisory committee (which includes a writer, two publishers, a literary agent, a bookseller, a librarian, and a chairperson appointed by the Booker Prize Foundation), and a judging panel (selected from leading literary critics, writers, academics and public figures), but many writers, critics and other interests parties question the very concept of a "best book" being chosen by a small number of literary insiders. It led *The Guardian* newspaper to introduce a "Not the Booker Prize", voted for by readers.

The judging process for this, and other awards, has also been criticised and questioned, as has the very idea that books can be compared and a winner selected. Can a 'book of the year' really be assessed annually by a bunch of people who have to read large numbers of entries at speed? Is this really the best way to honour a writer?

Other award controversies expose why awards should not to be taken all that seriously by authors. In 2016, two right-wing anti-diversity voting campaign groups called "The Sad Puppies" and "The Rabid Puppies" gamed the Hugo Awards to ensure Chuck Tingle's short story was nominated. Tingle writes in a very niche area—erotic gay stories, gay monster erotica, dinosaur erotica, etc.—with names like *Space Raptor Butt Invasion,* [1] which are far from typical Hugo Award stories. The politically motivated groups were successful in their bid, and two of Tingle's stories were short-listed two years' running.

In late 2019 through early 2020, RWA was swept up in controversy around its policies, practices, and behaviors in relation to widespread racism.

A lack of diversity in publishing—let alone awards—is not uncommon. So many voices aren't heard or appreciated because they come from another worldview, culture, or perspective than those who run the awards. It's a tragedy, really, when awarding bodies could use their power and potential to actually elevate authors from different backgrounds and voices. For the very first time in 2020, a woman of color won the British Book Award. The women's book prize was born out of the fact that there were so few women on major prize lists.

Sometimes a book wins a prize because it's a challenging type of book, but that doesn't necessarily mean that people end up loving it or regarding it as one of their favorites. In fact, sometimes winning a prize can actually result in your getting a lot of bad reviews, because it opens your book up to readers who wouldn't have necessarily found it through regular marketing, and they aren't your target market. If an awarding body says it's a great book and then you get a lot of reviews saying, "don't believe the hype," it can damage your book's reputation. It's an outrage really. There are so many readers in the world who seek out thousands of niche categories on digital bookstores. So really, who is to judge what determines greatness? There are niches because readers demand them. If your readers are satisfied, then surely that's a great book!

While winning a prize is a great honor, having readers love our books is the ultimate goal because it leads to long-term writing careers and success.

Awards, and award controversies, help to take books out into the wider world of mainstream discussion, to get people talking about books — and buying a few too.

Key Takeaways

For the indie author, book awards matter because:

- Book awards indicate a book's "worth" to the buying public and can boost book sales.
- Announcements of award long lists, short lists, and winners provide priceless publicity for the selected authors.
- You can enter the right award for *your* book to increase your chances of winning.

- Controversies surrounding certain awards don't negate the accolades of other book awards.
- Raving fans who love our books is the ultimate book award —and awards can help.

---

1. http://www.thehugoawards.org/hugo-history/2016-hugo-awards/

3

OPENING UP TO INDIE AUTHORS

I t is only when all the major national and international awards are truly inclusive that good writing of all kinds can compete fairly and equally.

When we first wrote about this topic back in 2013, the Folio Prize, now known as the Rathbones Folio Prize, had just launched. The prize was the first major literary award that consciously opened its doors to indies. and its first short-list in 2014 included Sergio De La Pava's originally self-published *A Naked Singularity*. The award is now also opening up to nonfiction and digital-only novels.

After a 56-year wait, the Romantic Novelists' Association Awards have now been open for several years to both self-published and trade-published authors. In 2017, Kate Johnson was named winner of the first Paranormal or Speculative Romantic Novel Award for *Max Seventeen*, making her the first self-published author in the award's history to win one of the prestigious RoNAs.

In 2021 the Young Writer of the Year doubled its first prize to £10,000. Many of the prize's winners, like Max Porter and Jay Bernard, have won for works that push the boundaries of genre and form. Given the prominence of young indie authors among the new generation of Instagram poets and in other digital-first formats, this award possibly remains the most promising contender to be first to see a major award for an indie writer.

Slightly disappointingly, the number of indie entries remains low, something ALLi has been working to reverse. There are many reasons why this may be the case, but possibly one of the most significant is that for the new generation of indie writers who cut their teeth on social media, such as the many following in the steps of the breakout Instapoet Rupi Kaur, instant recognition from peers matters more than institutional recognition.

For those not in the 18–35 category, the McKitterick Prize, which has a substantial prize pot and is open to debut writers over 40, also welcomes indies. Another such award, the Betty Trask, became the first to reward a self-published author when Kathleen Jowitt won a Betty Trask Award in 2017 for *Speak Its Name*.

Other recent new awards, newly stating that they are open to all authors regardless of how their books are published, are the Arnold Bennett Prize, the Jhalak Prize and the Polaris (The Polari First Book Prize, established in 2011, awarded annually for a first book which explores the LGBTQ+ experience. And established in 2019, The Polari Prize,awarded annually for a book by a a non-debut writer.)

We've seen the crowdfunding publishing platform Unbound hit the Booker shortlist with Paul Kingsnorth's *The Wake*. For two years in a row, in 2015 and 2016, the same tiny press, Oneworld, has published the winner. The Booker Prize has since opened its entries to include those from the USA.

Indie authors, though, are still not eligible. The Booker Prize is one of too many awards and prizes that have entry clauses like this, specifically designed to knock author-publishers out of the running.

"Self-published books are not eligible where the author is the publisher or where a company has been specifically set up to publish that book."

Opening Up to Indies

The experience of small independent presses is in many ways an excellent illustration and template, both for self-publishing writers and for prize organizers. The 2012 Man Booker Prize was a watershed moment for indie publishers. The prize had attracted a lot of negative attention in 2011 following remarks by judges that they were looking for "readable" books. The shortlist of 2012 went a long way toward silencing the critics, and the inclusion of books from small presses such as Salt Publishing's *The Lighthouse* and *Swimming Home* were an important part of this.

The case was made unequivocally for the literary quality of the work being published by small presses as well as the centrality of small presses among the best of contemporary literature. Since then, small presses are regularly represented on prize lists.

Why then are self-publishing authors dismissed for no apparent reason other than a pre-formed bias? It seems reasonable that all books, however they are produced, should be compared on an equal basis for what they say and how they say it, rather than whether their author or a 3rd party did the publishing.

Often the claim is that their "systems" couldn't cope with the number of entries. That they are afraid of being inundated with unsuitable material. That they want the curation that as publisher has already done.

On his blog, *A World Of Writers And Readers,* ALLi member Karl Drinkwater addressed the eligibility rules for the Wales Book of the Year competition run by Literature Wales in this light, and concluded:

"Do non-discriminatory prizes get too many entries? No. Can the level of entries be managed? Of course.

An insider told me it's really not hard to do; the Folio prize starts with a form submission about the book and goes from there...

Also, if an organization is worried about the number of entries, it can implement quality controls. This is far better than arbitrary exclusions. Apply the same criteria to all books, trade published or independent.

Personally, I'd exclude books with more than one typo or error (grammatical, printing, formatting): That would get the list down pretty quickly, without prejudice. But they could be more lenient than me and still have a manageable list with poor-quality works excluded."

— KARL DRINKWATER

Another serious obstacle that existed when we first wrote about it in *Open Up to Indie Authors* many years ago has been removed for many prizes (though not all): publishers having to pay large sums if their books were short-listed for any of the major awards. This had disastrous consequences for many small presses, who would often have to either sell a successful title or enter a partnership with a larger press to secure funding in order to enter their books.

Thankfully, this was changed by many award committees, including the Man-Booker, as a result of a successful campaign led by Sam Jordison of Galley Beggars Press.

Attitude or Awareness or Availability

Besides the unnecessary entry clauses that limit availability for an indie, there are perhaps other reasons for the low number of self-published entries for literary awards.

"One of the main reasons we're not seeing indies winning traditional awards," says ALLi's news editor and co-author of the *Opening Up to Indie Authors* guidebook, Dan Holloway, "is that indies simply aren't entering."

The reasons are many. Perhaps we assume too quickly that we are not eligible for the big prizes. Or maybe we aim our sights too low by what we perceive to be more achievable goals: smaller, lesser-known, and specialist prizes. For some it's a lack of awareness or thinking their work isn't good enough For others, it's a lack of time or interest. Still others consider the ideas of awards for writing invidious, or are put off by the widely known controversies surrounding some of the awards programs.

ALLi recommends dabbling in local contests as well to spread your reach and boost your confidence, especially when just starting out—but also encourages authors to be bold and enter suitable books for the more prestigious prizes.

We also need more awareness of award opportunities for indies. An interesting coda here comes from speaking to the organizers of one of the prizes that has not only opened its doors, but has actively sought out indies, and made a big deal of its openness. The Peters Fraser + Dunlop Young Writer of the Year award is worth £5,000 to the winner and has in the past been won by such luminaries as Sarah Waters and Zadie Smith. When the prize was relaunched in 2015 after a hiatus since 2009, it was made open to self-published titles.

ALLi promoted the event, and Dan Holloway attended a special event for bloggers to help spread the word, but there were still very few self-published entrants. So it's not just that prizes that need to be more open to indies, but that *more indies need to submit to prizes*. Some of the success stories are inspiring.

Jamaican author Ezekel Alan almost didn't enter his self-published debut novel *Disposable People* for the Commonwealth Book Prize 2013, for which he was named a Regional Winner.

"My first novel was written almost as a process of catharsis or perhaps exorcism, getting rid of some old ghosts from the past. A major national newspaper back home thought of it differently, however, and gave it rave reviews. Then the person who edited the book, a Brit, pointed out to me that the Commonwealth Book Prize was now open to self-published novels. I had known of the Commonwealth Book Prize before, but never once thought that my act of exorcism would even remotely be worthy of consideration for that award. The novel was entered, and became the first self-published book to win a major international prize. The publicity which ensued was overwhelming."

— Ezekel Alan

Irish children's author Benji Bennett, by contrast, now takes entering awards in stride, winning the children's category of the Bord Gáis Energy Irish Book Awards not once, but twice, most recently in 2013, for *When You Were Born*. Reporting about the award on his Independent Publishing Magazine blog, Mick Rooney wrote:

> "Ireland's premier national book award is unusual in that, unlike other prestigious book awards, it does not preclude self-published titles from being nominated, requiring only that a title should be written by an Irish author, published within the year of the awards, and in print and available through Irish book wholesalers. Titles are nominated and voted on equally by a panel of book industry experts and public online voting... This is actually Benji Bennett's second time to win the Children's Category Award (first in 2009) having self-published seven books since 2008."
>
> — Mick Rooney

These examples are but some of many other prestigious book awards around the world, albeit with smaller purses and wider remits than the big three.

Indie authors should feel free to enter their books, if they are confident that the award is appropriate to their work and their book is of a suitable category and standard. Unless a rule specifically excludes self-published authors, the choice is yours. For some time to come, every such award won will be a victory not only for the author, but for the cause of self-published authors everywhere.

So Good They Can't Ignore You

No self-published author has yet been awarded any of the big three literary awards: the Pulitzer, The Booker Prize, or the Nobel Prize for Literature, though one did come close. Jill Paton Walsh was way ahead of her time in the self-publishing revolution when she made the short-list of the then Booker Prize in 1994 with *Knowledge of Angels*.

"My third adult novel was rejected by the publisher of the first two and I could not understand the criticism offered... the book in question, *Knowledge of Angels*, felt to me like the one I was born to write."

— PATON WALSH

Paton-Walsh's agent did succeed in licensing it to Houghton Mifflin in the US but, try as they might, they couldn't find a UK publisher. Before publication day, her US editor phoned: did she want a few extra copies so her British friends could read it? "The nineteenth London rejection was on my desk," says Paton Walsh. "My husband said: 'Fuck them all – we'll do it ourselves.' We rang back and said: 'Can you make that 1,000?' In a burst of furious activity we got an ISBN, mocked up a British title page and swift-aired the books across the Atlantic." With the help of indie publisher friends, they organized a sales rep, an invoicing programme, a warehouse, and a publicist.

The book was distributed and began to sell in significant numbers for a literary philosophical novel. It went into reprint, foreign rights began to sell, and Transworld bought the paperback rights. And then it made the longlist for the 1994 Booker Prize. And then the shortlist.

"I didn't win the Booker, but by then I really didn't need to; our action in self-publishing the book in Britain was vindicated."

— PATON WALSH

(You can read her account of her achievement in The Guardian.[1])

At that time, author-publishing was available only to a limited number of lucky authors with specialist knowledge. Now that the digital revolution has changed everything about self-publishing, it can only be a matter of time before another indie author's book is long-listed, short-listed, and declared the winner.

There is a key point here that indie authors need to take on board. It comes down to that old adage: Make yourself so good they can't ignore you. When a book comes along that is truly brilliant, and the prize that should have been its natural home has no choice but to reject it, that's when pressure will prise open the doors. It has happened in science fiction. Sadly, it hasn't happened with general or literary fiction. Yet. For some organizations, it may take time to change rules that have long been in place.

Key Takeaways

In summary, interested indie authors should:

- Be aware that some entry clauses are designed to eliminate self-published authors.
- Not assume their books are ineligible or not "good enough" to win.
- Expand their awareness of the myriad awards and contests that are available.
- Make their work so good that it can't be ignored.

1. https://www.theguardian.com/lifeandstyle/2010/oct/24/jill-paton-walsh-a-life

4

PRIZES EXCLUSIVE TO INDIE AUTHORS

I n contrast to the variable treatment of indie authors in large mainstream awards, there is now a proliferation of smaller awards for self-published books. There are also lots of awards limited *only* to self-published books. Good news? Yes and no.

Such awards can be the real deal, run by a dedicated individual or group, determined to amplify good indie writing and publishing. Or they can be money-making schemes, run by scam merchants, whose only interest is in maximising entries. And everything in between.

The money-making awards often have numerous genre categories and high entry fees, both of which suggest a primary concern with maximizing entry income over the publicity for authors. Smaller awards, both well-meaning and money-driven, can come and go very quickly.

ALLi believes the rewards to the authors should be first and foremost, rather than to just their organizers.

Two particular awards have raised the profile of prizes aimed specifically at self-published books. Namely the "Selfies" and Amazon's "Kindle Storyteller Award."

The "Selfies" were launched at London Book Fair in 2019. The following year, as all such events moved online, the "Selfies" expanded, running at both the virtual London Book Fair and the last-ever BookExpo. ALLi's Jane Davis won the first award with the novel *Smash All the Windows*. When the categories were expanded in 2020 to include children's as well as adult fiction, both winners, Jemma Hatt and Clare Flynn, were ALLi members. For 2021, the awards have expanded yet again, this time to include memoir.

Many authors have entered the Amazon Breakthrough Novel Award over the years. The "Kindle Storyteller Award," by contrast, is for already completed works. Launched in 2017, it comes with a huge £20,000 first prize. The model is a familiar one in the prize world. A list of star judges selects the winner, but from a shortened list that is compiled for them—in this case through an algorithm that mixes, among other things, sales and reviews.

Publishers' Weekly has established the BookLife Prize. This is part of a move by the company to pay more attention to self-publishing. *Publishers' Weekly* has also moved into the event space created by the demise of BookExpo. And where BookExpo had seen its support for indies dwindle, the new event from *Publishers' Weekly* promises us a more central role.

Sadly, the prize seems to be going down some of the less-promising roads of other similar awards. BookLife is *Publishers' Weekly's* self-publishing "section" (backwater). Entries to the $5,000 prize will have to have been featured in that section of the publication. And the only way to guarantee that is to buy a paid review.

As indie authors, we're susceptible to those who take advantage of our legitimate wish to expand our impact and influence, as writers and as publishers. Being an indie author is hard work, and it's wonderful when somebody recognizes your book but lots of the awards and prizes that are directed toward indie authors are completely useless, for the writer. They're just money-making schemes for the unscrupulous.

At a time when some of the bigger prizes for traditionally published books are shaking off the disincentives, many new self-publishing specific prizes seem to be stuck with them.

It is down to the individual author to seek out the awards they feel best fit their work in terms of territory, genre, and attitude, and also to decide when it's better to walk away rather than to submit their book for an unworthy award.

Before proceeding with entering an awards program or contest, ascertain whether the award program you wish to enter is charging a reasonable and affordable fee in relation to any benefits that winning might yield. Are the costs balanced by the benefits?

If you think yes, then examine the program's marketing materials; that is, its website, the awards it offers, its promotional activity, its author recognition. Does it look professional? An amateurish award logo won't do your book or your author website any favors. In fact, it does the opposite.

Hannah Jacobson, founder of BookAwardPro.com said this in a recent ALLi blog post:

"When evaluating an award program, consider emailing the award to get a feel for their customer service. We find that behind the screen, there are good people wanting to do good work for authors, and friendly customer service tends to be an easy way to spot a great program.

Additionally, perform a litmus test: while reading the award website, does it seem respectful of authors? Does the program value what awards can do for authors (and not the other way around)?"

— HANNAH JACOBSON

Finally, if the program passes those tests, take time to research previous winners. Have you heard of them? If not, look them up on Amazon. Take a "look inside" their books, and read their reviews. Does what you see align with their status as an award-winning author? If not, it is reasonable to assume that the award is a scam to extract money from naïve newbie authors. Click away, and move on.

ALLi Book Awards Watchdog

As part of its community outreach program, ALLi's watchdog desk provides a ratings page for contests and awards. Monitored by watchdog John Doppler and ALLi director Orna Ross, our ratings dashboard now has over 120 entries rated under three categories, recommended, mixed, and caution.

Guiding Principles

rates awards based on the following guiding principles.

1. The event should exist to recognize talent, not to enrich the organizers. Avoid events driven by excessive entry fees, marketing services to entrants, or selling merchandise such as stickers and certificates.
2. Receiving an award should be a significant achievement. An event that hands out awards like Halloween candy dilutes the value of those awards. Beware of events that offer awards in dozens of categories. These are often schemes to maximize the number of winners in order to sell them stickers and other merchandise.
3. The judging process should be transparent and clear. Watch out for contests if the judging criteria and personnel are vague or undisclosed.
4. Prizes should be appropriate and commensurate with the entry fees collected. If a cash prize is offered, it should offer a reasonable return on the entry fee. "Exposure" is not an appropriate prize. Representation or publication are acceptable prizes, but only if offered by a reputable company without hidden fees.
5. Entrants should not be required to forfeit key rights to their work.

The fact that award programs charge for entry should not be a deterrent. It is not unreasonable to ask entrants who are taking a small punt on winning to contribute to the considerable costs of running such a program. After all, it is you, not the organizers of the award program, who will ultimately profit from increased sales if you win. That is why many major awards can only operate by attracting commercial sponsors that invest in the author program in return for publicity for their own business.

It is impossible for ALLi to keep up with all the award programs out there, so you need to develop your own ability to know whether an awards program is legitimate or profiteering.

ALLi is willing to work with any award or contest that wants to open up to indie authors. We also wish to hear feedback from authors who have entered contests and awards. Please contact John Doppler at the Watchdog Desk at any time if you would like to inform us about a contest or award or discuss a rating: John@allianceindependentauthors.org

---

Key Takeaways

Prizes that are exclusive to indie authors should benefit the authors first and foremost, rather than to just their organizers.

Don't be fooled by well-known brand names

If in doubt, consult ALLi's Awards & Contest Ratings Page. See SelfPublishingAdvice.org/awards.

5

VANITY AWARDS & ANTHOLOGIES
SPOTTING QUESTIONABLE AWARDS

I f you do decide to submit your work for awards, proceed with caution. Otherwise, you may do more harm than good, both to your own reputation and to that of the self-publishing movement as a whole.

The first thing you need to do is rule out awards that are run by unscrupulous or profiteering organizers. There are a number of identifiers of questionable and profiteering awards.

No Reputation. When you search the awards program online, all you get is their own website. There is no mention of them in any other media.

Anonymous judging. Award programs always promise selection and judging by publishing experts of high standing, but profiteering awards rarely reveal names, because these "experts" don't exist.

High entry fees and low prize money. Profiteering awards generally charge $50 and upwards to enter your book. They also offer early bird and other entry options that are all about maximising profits.

Numerous entry categories. Profiteering awards create as many entry categories as possible, and encourage multiple entries across categories.

Non-prize prizes. Profiteering awards offer prizes that cost them little or nothing: press releases, media announcements, database and website listings, features on satellite websites or in self-owned publications, digital seals, badges and certificates.

Opportunities to spend more money. The most profiteering awards charge for these "prizes": stickers, seals for your book, certificates, reviews and more.

Solicitation. It's common for independent authors to receive an email saying, "We've read your book and it's fabulous, and we want to enter it for such and such an award... the fee is such and such." If you receive an email like this, please do not respond or be pulled in by it. While these emails can seem legitimate, and may even have a nice website set up with testimonials and kudos, they are usually insidious. Just as legitimate publishers don't solicit authors to send manuscripts, legitimate prize programs don't ask authors to enter. An out-of-the-blue email saying your book has been selected for an awards program should be dispatched to your spam folder.

Not all the problem awards tick all these boxes, for examples. Some legitimate awards may tick one or two, not yet having established a reputation, for example. However, if a number of these are present in a contest or awards program, though, and especially if the entry fees are sizeable, move along.

Vanity Anthologies

On the popular Writers Beware[1] website, publishing industry watchdog Victoria Strauss adds a warning about vanity anthologies, another way in which unscrupulous companies make money out of authors' hunger for publication. The most common vanity anthology scheme is a "contest", inviting writers to "enter" poems or stories. Then they are told they've "won" a place, and pressured to buy lots of copies and invite other buyers who will be so proud of their "achievement".

These collections of poems, short stories, or essay are not produced for, or distributed to, any readers beyond the contributors to the anthology, and their family and friends.

Sometimes publication is contingent on purchase of the anthology and sometimes it isn't, but either way, writers are pressured to buy multiple copies. Because inclusion in these anthologies is offered to almost everyone who enters, an anthology-published poem or story isn't a legitimate literary credit.

— VICTORIA STRAUSS

Another vanity anthology scheme is the pay-to-play anthology, whereby writers pay upfront for inclusion in the anthology, as well as buying large numbers of the books, and other merchandise, on publication.

Strauss cites the *Wake Up...Live the Life You Love* anthologies, which require contributors to buy up to 500 books at a cost of several thousand dollars, and boasts that its anthologies include articles by such well-known figures as Dr. Wayne Dyer and Tony Robbins. The series owner has bought a license to re-use). The anthologies, published by Inspired Living Publishing, expect contributors to also pay for marketing packages and dubious promotional products.

Nonfiction pay-to-play anthologies tout themselves as an opportunity for entrepreneurs and business owners to enhance their professional images by presenting themselves as published authors and using the anthology as a kind of business card. For someone with plenty of money to spare, might this be a reasonable form of publicity? Possibly, given that the general public has no idea that these schemes exist and won't know you bought your publishing credit, and assuming that the anthologies are professionally produced and edited (not a guarantee--this is definitely a case of try before you buy), and that the anthology company will actually send you the books you purchase.

But if you're seriously considering paying for something like this, ask yourself whether it's worth laying out several thousand dollars just to be able to say you got published in an anthology series no one ever heard of--and whether you really want several hundred books that you'll either have to hustle to sell, or stuff in a dark corner of your basement.

Ultimately, of course, the award that matters most of all is great feedback that is unsolicited from loyal readers, not the paid-for endorsements by charlatans that no one has ever heard of—least of all, the readers you are targeting.

The most useful thing that can be said to authors considering applying for a quality control award is to search ALLi's Services Watchdog ratings and reports[2]. And if the service you are investigating doesn't appear, drop the watchdog a note so the team can perform their due diligence before you apply.

Key Takeaways

Before entering a contest, you should:

- Disregard unsolicited emails that praise your book and offers to enter your book into an award program.
- Check out ALLi's Ratings service that indicates whether each of 120 award listings is recommended, mixed, or cautioned against.
- Learn how to assess an award program by paying attention to red flags
- Be aware of anthology "contests" and pay-to-play anthology schemes

---

1. https://www.sfwa.org/other-resources/for-authors/writer-beware/contests/
2. https://selfpublishingadvice.org/author-awards-contests-rated-reviewed/

6

OTHER AWARD FORMATS & GENRES

L arge prestigious book prizes aren't the only game in awards
town. There are a great many others awards, organised around
different criteria, including quality control awards, readers' choice
awards and awards for specific genres.

Quality Control Awards

Book awards that single out winners from the pack are not to be
confused with the quality control awards offered by book evaluation
sites such as Awesome Indies and Indie BRAG. These organizations
judge books not against each other, but against professional standards
of publication. For readers who are wary of self-published authors,
these can provide useful reassurance. For authors, they provide third-
party endorsement and a confidence boost.

They also draw attention to the fact that a book has been self-
published. Their badge of approval can therefore be displayed on a
book jacket not only as a sign that the content is of a
professional standard, but also as a proud assertion of the author's
self-published status.

In the past few years, awards of this kind have proliferated as more and more indies look for ways to validate the professional approach they have taken in the eyes of their readers. With such a growing demand comes an inevitable range of standards in the expanding market to meet it.

Dublin Literary Award

The Dublin Literary Award is presented annually for a novel written in English or translated into English, awarding "excellence in world literature". It's worth mentioning for its unique nomination process.

Solely sponsored by Dublin City Council, and administered by Dublin City Libraries, nominations are made by libraries in capital and major cities around the world. Participating libraries can nominate up to one novel each year.

Over 400 library systems in 177 countries worldwide are invited to nominate books each year, with Dublin City Libraries actively seeking out and encouraging nominations from countries that have not previously nominated.

Indie authors interested in this award need to focus on making sure their books are distributed and lent in libraries around the world and form a relationship with a participating library willing to nominate their book.

Audiobook Awards

While it is frustrating to observe how little has opened up to indie authors since we first started monitoring awards, audiobooks are the big exception.

The sector has seen double-digit growth consistently for years now, and the rise of subscription services is currently fuelling even more growth. Platforms like ACX and Findaway Voices have made it easier for indies to produce our own audiobooks and that has opened up the possibility of indie authors winning the Audiobook Publishers' Awards. The "Audies," as they are popularly known, used to be the domain of publishers with the budget it took to produce high-ticket audiobooks. This it is now not only technically open, but affordable, for author-publishers.

Podium Publishing, a leading independent publisher of audiobooks, won its first Audie Award Thursday when it picked up the originally self-published *The Martian*, a *New York Times* and audible.com bestselling book written and published by Andy Weir.

There are also the Independent Audiobook Awards, where indie authors show their prizewinning publishing prowess beside other small- and micro-publishers.

Poetry and Short Story Awards

Poetry and short stories have always had a large number of high-profile awards. Many of the awards for single poems and single stories also have an "open to anyone" policy. This means that indies, traditionally published, hybrid, and totally unpublished writers have always shared the spoils.

Many of the most prestigious short story awards e.g. the Commonwealth Writers' Prize are open to all, but unfortunately, the same award doors that were closed in 2013 when ALLi first addressed the issue remain closed today. In the UK, the National Short Story Award, which has a huge £15,000 first prize, remains closed to anyone who has not been traditionally published. The same is true of poetry awards, despite the meteoric rise of self-published digital poetry, led by instapoets like Rupi Kaur and Atticus.

It is hard to understand how this kind of restriction can still be justified, given that IngramSpark's founder Robin Cutler has pointed up that poetry is the distributor's bestselling print book genre.

Readers Choice Awards

A reader's choice award is just what it says, an award given to a book that is chosen by readers, most often in online poll voting, but chosen in other ways too. The UK *Books Are My Bag Readers Awards*, for example, are mostly curated by bookshops and chosen by readers. Booksellers across the UK and Ireland curate six shortlists, while the

Readers' Choice Award is nominated and chosen entirely by readers. In Chapter one, we heard of The Guardian newspaper's Not The Booker prize, voted by readers.

The biggest and best known readers choice award program is the Goodreads Choice Awards. Goodreads is a popular (Amazon owned) social media platform for book-lovers, where they can share their books and reviews. Many publishers and author-publishers use the platform promote their works.

In 2009, the platform started hosting the Goodreads Choice Awards, a selection of the best titles chosen by its users. Each year, Goodreads nominates 15 books in each of 20 genre categories by analyzing statistics from millions of book ratings added throughout the year on their site, as well as write-in nominations. Goodreads members then have a set amount of days each year to vote for their favorite books. The winner becomes the Goodreads Choice of the year in that genre category.

Children's Book Awards

There are a vast number of children's book awards, recognising outstanding authors and illustrators that provide outstanding reading experiences for young people. They differ a little from adult books, in that the reader is not the buyer, so awards in this category are for books of that are purchased largely by teachers, parents and other relatives.

Many children's book awards, though not all, are selected by librarians. Award-winners then get orders from libraries and bookstores. Like award winning books for adults, those for children tend to be more prominently displayed in bookstores and to stay in print longer.

For writers and illustrators, getting to know the award-winning books is a way to absorb what is considered to be the best in children's books today, rather than 20 or 30 or 40 years ago, when we were children. Some awards even say they exist to encourage teachers to increase their professional and personal knowledge of recently published, high-quality children's books.

The children's book genre also has its own readers' choice awards, the Children's Book Award. Voted for solely by children from start to finish, it's highly regarded by parents, teachers, librarians, publishers and children's authors and illustrators, as it truly does represent the childrens' choice. Publishers support this prize by donating around 800 new books each year to be read and reviewed by Testing Groups across the UK each year, with over 100,000 total votes being cast in the process. At the end of each testing year, the books are donated to hospitals, women's refuges, nurseries and disadvantaged schools by the CBA groups.

Grants and Foundations

Many grants and foundations remain closed to independent authors. The UK Royal Literary Fund, for example, which funds writers who are suffering financial hardship "and have had several works published in the UK for a general readership" rules out books where , publication was subsided by the writer or others, and explicitly says "self-published authors are ineligible for this funding".

An ALLi member who has been frustrated by such exclusions is Lorna Fergusson, who questions the allocation of grants and funds by the Society of Authors, of which she is a member and supporter. "It's ironic to see their latest advert on Facebook (and in their member magazine *The Author*), promoting 'Funding for authors, to buy time, and aid research.'" One of these funds is the Authors' Foundation, which offers money to help with research and travel. Fergusson continues:

"The wording of this grant starts by saying that 'Any published author working on a full-length book for a British publisher who needs funding is welcome to apply.' Later it adds 'Without a contractual commitment by a publisher you may apply so long as you have had at least one book published and there is a strong likelihood that your next book will be published.'

Immediately I see issues with this because it is not clear what constitutes a "published author" or "a publisher" here. It does not allow for the fluid state of such definitions in the current publishing industry. I, as a self-published author, am a publisher, using my own Fictionfire Press imprint, for instance.

I have quoted here from The Author. The Facebook advert goes further, adding:

'Please note, we are unable to accept self-published authors as grants cannot be awarded to help towards the costs of publication. Grants cannot be made for education or research costs.'"

— LORNA FERGUSSON

This rejection was especially galling to Fergusson as it came in the wake of her ineligibility to apply for a British Library residency that included access to the library's special collections and was open to writers working on books set in America or Canada. It seemed ideal for her book, The Concealment, set in Canada amongst other locations.

This work already had prize-winning potential—the opening of that novel was awarded first prize in the Words with Jam First Page competition. She was disappointed to find, on further investigation, that she was not eligible.

"It turned out that this residency was only available to those who already had a contract to publish the book. How can you have the contract if the book is not yet written because you haven't done the research, which is why you're applying for assistance to carry out said research? How is this practicable for anyone who is writing their book on spec and has not signed a two-book contract?

"It's the same kind of paradox I've noted with the Society of Authors: a trumpeting of the values of freedom and open-mindedness and encouragement negated by an outdated sense of exclusivity. They have added that you must now have evidence of a contract and publishing schedule and say, 'We do not accept self-published authors of any kind,' which is a shocker of a phrase."

— LORNA FERGUSSON

The exclusions around administration of grants were brought home during the Covid-19 crisis of 2020. Hardship funds for the creative arts from the governments around the world included funds for writers, administered by national author associations. To the best of ALLi's knowledge at the time of writing, using information gathered from publicly available lists of awards made, indie authors have not received *any* of these funds.

The Society of Authors says it does not set the rules of these awards, it just administers the funds, and wants to support its self-publishing members. The Young Writer of the Year is a prime example of a shift at the SoA, with organizers now not only welcoming indie authors, but consulting with ALLi on how to attract the best indie entrants.

Key Takeaways

In summary, targeted awards can help the indie author stand out in different ways:

- Quality Control Awards provide a badge of approval and is a sign that the content is professional.
- Audiobook Awards reflect the double-digit growth of the market and is a wide open possibility for indies.
- Many poetry and short story awards are open to indie writers and offer significant prizes and recognition for the writers.

7

ENTERING AWARDS

FURTHER ADVICE

One of the most important aspects of becoming an effective author-publisher is knowing your comparison authors and titles, as well as the current common tropes, themes, or elements of the genre you write in. You simply cannot deliver a genre-specific book without understanding the reader requirements for that genre. (And yes, literary fiction authors, you too write within a genre).

It's exactly the same for awards and contests. You need to ensure your book is a match for that award. Sacha Black, ALLi's Blog Manager, was on the Amazon Kindle Storyteller Judging panel in 2020. She said this:

"The Kindle Storyteller Award panel are looking for a book that is heavily story driven. While the overall package is taken into consideration, it's the story that grips you and won't let you go until it's done that is going to be the winner. Unlike, say, the Pulitzer winner which is going to require an insane level of depth and indulgent prose and other such qualities."

— SACHA BLACK

Unless you have read, re-read, and fully understood the requirements for whatever you're entering, you can't possibly deliver a winning book. Winners meet specific criteria, and the criteria is there because the judges have something specific they're after.

Entry Requirements

It's simply a given that any author should check the entry requirements of any award or prize, and yet hundreds of authors simply don't.

Annie Mydla, from Winning Writers and judge for the North Street Book Prize, said this in a recent ALLi blog post:

"In our last contest, we refunded nearly 100 entry fees for books that didn't meet our guidelines. This happens most in our Creative Nonfiction & Memoir category, where we regularly get entries that are specifically excluded in the rules: biographies, history books, self-help, and religious tracts, to name a few. If it's unclear if your book is eligible, please ask. This helps us clarify our rules, and sometimes we add a category when we see interest. An example is our Art Book category added just this year."

— ANNIE MYDLA

But it isn't just genre criteria that authors miss, it's formatting guidelines, word count guidelines, and information requirements, too.

Always, always, always check the requirements. And then recheck them for good measure. You don't want your manuscript eliminated due to a missed entry requirement or technical instruction.

Take time too to read previous winners' books to understand the "feel" and tone of winners. There is often a style, voice, or feel that competitions are looking for.

For example, Annie Mydla, Judge for the North Street Book Prize said:

"Let your book communicate something beyond mere knowledge of its plot and characters. Entries that make my short-list don't just focus on what happened and to whom, but leave the reader with a new knowledge of deep social, psychological, and spiritual truths. The plot and characters are not the only level of engagement— North Street winners also give readers a profound sense of having come in touch with new ways of thinking and existing."

— ANNIE MYDLA

IT GOES WITHOUT SAYING THAT YOU SHOULD HAVE WORKED ON YOUR craft. Your manuscript should have had feedback, been polished by professional editors, and been proofread by an expert before it's submitted for entry.

Submit Standalone Books

In an ALLi podcast, Joanna Penn in discussion with Orna Ross noted the general preference for standalone books over series books for competition entries:

"I'm about to write book 12 in a series and look, to be honest, you're pleasing your existing readership with a book in a long series. You're not writing a book that you're aiming to necessarily win a prize with."

— JOANNA PENN

Orna replied stating:

"I agree with you… think about the judge reading. They're unlikely to know anything about your work because, oftentimes, everything but the title and your content has been stripped away. They won't know who the author is or what happened in the rest of the series. It has to be a really pleasing experience to read that book, and if it's part of a series, it can work as a standalone within a series, but that's not the same thing as something that creates a complete world beginning to end. And you want, as a judge, to feel that overwhelming satisfaction at the end of the read."

— ORNA ROSS

Joanna continued providing a fantastic example of a winning standalone book:

"Look at the Bram Stoker award… A few years ago, Christopher Golden won with his book *Ararat,* which is a perfect example of the genre. I read this book, and every single thing about this book was brilliant in terms of being a perfect example of the genre, yet still original. That originality, the "something different" is so important. It can't be the 79th psychological thriller in a series you've written with a female first-person viewpoint, you know?"

— JOANNA PENN

Some Final "Before You Enter" Warnings

When you find an award that seems a good match for your work, don't rush in. Read the submission guidelines and entry requirements carefully, and work out exactly how much it will cost you. This may be more than is immediately evident. For example, if you have to send a quantity of print books in addition to the entry fee, be sure to include the money spent for printing the books and the price of shipping in your calculations.

One well-known online award program specifically for self-published books requires a $75 fee per entry in a single category (add another $50 per additional category), plus the submission of two print books (add your print and shipping costs for these). There are sixty categories, and many books would fall into more than one. Although there are a handful of larger prizes, the first prize in each category is just $100, a medal, a certificate, and a number of stickers for your books. How many stickers? Five. If you want more, you have to pay for them. Oh, and there's an invitation to attend an awards ceremony in New York. Undoubtedly, you will bear the cost for that, too.

There appears to be no shortage of entrants in this particular program. Many of the top prize winners have fewer than 20 reviews each on Amazon.com, some not flattering. Along the same vein as Michael N. Marcus's declaration on the ALLi blog that every book can now be a bestseller if put in a sufficiently rarefied category, *every* book can win a prize—provided that the author is prepared to pay for entry to enough indiscriminate award schemes.

Key Takeaways

In summary, you should only enter a contest:

- If it abides by the Guiding Principles highlighted by ALLi's Watchdog Team
- You have researched it thoroughly, including entry guidelines, eligibility, fees, and if it's the right award for your book.
- After following all the entry requirements and instructions precisely so your manuscript is not eliminated.
- By submitting a standalone alone book rather than one that is part of a series.

8

JUDGING AWARDS

A s a successful indie author, you may well be approached to be a judge in a competition, prize, or award program. Having the opportunity to assess stories against required criteria can be a beneficial experience, both for your own writing and any future submissions you might make to awards yourself.

Most awards and competitions need lots of skilled readers to cover the slew of initial entries in order to determine the long-list or short-list. Some of these volunteer reader roles do require membership in an organization. For example, readers for The Bram Stoker award are expected to be members of the Horror Writers Association.

Orna Ross, ALLi Director, who no longer reads for awards but has judged a number of fiction and poetry awards in the past, says "reading brand new work hot off the creative presses is always an expansive experience. You learn so much from exposure to work that you probably wouldn't voluntarily choose to read, or even be aware of. Each award program has its own set of judging criteria, and so is enlightening in a different way. For example, the Dublin Literary Award promotes excellence in world literature while the Amazon Storyteller Awards is all about plot and meeting genre expectations.

It's hard work, reading lots of books under a tight deadline, and sometimes choosing a winner is difficult but I know that judging awards has made me a better writer and more aware of the qualities that make a book an award-winner."

Judging a book award forces you to read a lot over a focused period of time and also ensures you'll think critically about the books you're reading. There can only be one winner, so you have to constantly weigh whether one book is better than others in the category, and be able to justify your choices to the other judges on the panel.

Discussing shortlisted and nominated books with a group of strangers is also illuminating. You can't help but emerge from this process with a deeper understanding about what makes a book work.

In 2020, Sacha Black took over from Orna as the Alliance of Independent Authors representative on the Kindle Storyteller Awards panel. Sacha agrees that judging an awards is hard work but an opportunity worth taking.

"It was both an honor and a privilege to be on the Storyteller panel. Not only to be part of something so prestigious, but also because of how much I learnt. It was fascinating to see other judges' comments and viewpoints, where they matched mine and where they differed and why. But more importantly, it was eye-opening to see how my own mindset shifted once I was in the position of 'judge.'

"We get so close to our work that we can struggle to see the wood for the trees, but as a judge, you're really reminded of what a 'good' book looks like. You're also reminded of how important each individual element is and it forces you to be objective and critical—something I took back to my own work.

More than anything, though, I recognized what I *don't* like in stories and that has helped me eradicate such qualities from my own work. I encourage anyone wanting to win an award to volunteer to be a judge."

Like being a book club member, judging an award makes you read more widely. Rebecca J. Allen recalls how her first year reading for the Cybils Awards, a book bloggers' award program that aims to recognize the children's and young adult authors and illustrators whose books combine the highest literary merit and popular appeal, stretched her beyond her usual reading comfort zone. She was asked to judge the junior/senior high nonfiction category

I don't feel nonfiction is my strong suit, but I was pleasantly surprised by how much I enjoyed those books. Even once I moved to the spec fic category that lies closer to my heart, not every book on the list of nominees was one I would have pulled from a bookstore shelf. I found some unexpected book loves!

Joanna Penn, in a podcast with ALLi director Orna Ross, points up the particular value of judging an award in your own genre category. Writers are always told that one of the most important things they can do to improve their craft is to read. Specifically, to read in their genre and read critically. Judging an award forces you to do exactly that.

"I would urge authors who are part of a genre organization to volunteer, because they always need people to do the first round judging. It's hard work to assess hundreds of books in maybe six to eight months, but you very much get to see the standards of what's going on in your genre, and you get to learn what your taste is like, and cultural differences across your genre. As a British woman, I find a lot of the time I'm the only Brit, and the cultural taste differences are really interesting."

— JOANNA PENN

Finally, the process of reading gazillion books, whittling them down to a short-list and arguing their case will show you how subjective the market is. There's nothing like a heated book judging panel argument to demonstrate that no matter how good one savvy and experienced reader thinks a book is, another equally savvy and experienced reader very much disagrees.

Being a book award judge will show you, like nothing else, that we can't please everybody, no matter how well we write. As author-publishers, we must find and connect with the right readers for our own books.

Key Takeaways

In summary, you should consider volunteering as judge or reader because:

- Judging stories against eligibility criteria is hugely beneficial both for your own writing and any future awards you might enter.
- Volunteer readers for anthologies help the editor short-list down to a manageable list of stories to choose from.
- When you judge a book for its quality, you learn what a "good" book looks and reads like.
- Judging helps develop your critical eye, which helps you know how to better analyze your own work and understand your readership.

9

AUTHOR PREPARE

YOUR AWARD ENTRY CHECKLIST

Now that you know the ins and outs of author contests, awards, and prizes, maybe you're ready to give it a go for yourself. Here's a list of useful steps:

1. **Do Your Research:** Find out which awards are available to you as an indie author. There's a Contest Resources section at the end of this guidebook as well as many awards listed in previous chapters.
2. **Consider** volunteering to be a judge before entering any contests to familiarize yourself with the process and develop your critical eye.
3. **Examine** the pros and cons for you of entering an award contest, whether it's the controversies or the accolades or the cost of entry. Do what's right for you.
4. **Drill Deeper:** Find the award that fits perfectly for your book, genre, and niche.
5. **Start small** or pursue local contests to learn the process and build your confidence.
6. **Do Your Due Diligence**: Once you've narrowed your list of

awards, check out the ALLi Watchdog Desk for Awards Ratings. Avoid any award that is listed as "caution."

7. **Make sure** your manuscript is competition ready: have it professionally designed, formatted, edited, and proofread. Only submit your best work.
8. **Follow** the entry requirements and instructions to the letter.
9. **Submit** your manuscript and your entry form per the ground rules and deadline.
10. **Picture** yourself as an award-winning author!

THE END

RESOURCES

ALLi's awards and contests ratings desk
https://selfpublishingadvice.org/author-awards-contests-rated-reviewed/

ALLi BLOGS AND PODCASTS
Podcast with Joanna and Orna:
https://selfpublishingadvice.org/literary-prizes/

VICTORIA STRAUSS' BLOG POSTS
https://accrispin.blogspot.com/2015/06/awards-profiteers-how-writers-can.html
https://www.sfwa.org/other-resources/for-authors/writer-beware/contests/

AWARD SERVICES
BookAwardPro.com

ACKNOWLEDGMENTS

Alliance of Independent Authors (ALLi) guides rely heavily on the work and wisdom of our team, members, ambassadors and advisors. All of this is generously and freely shared with our non-profit CIC (Community Interest Company), with the intention of paying it forward, and benefitting other indie authors.

For this guide to becoming an award-winning author, particular thanks are due to ALLi news editor Dan Holloway, blog editor Sacha Black, and founder and CEO of ALLi Orna Ross. And Partner Member, Book Award Pro, a technology-enabled award submission service.

Thank you for your generosity and for lighting the way.

Thanks also to the creative team: publishing administrator Sarah Begley, editor Lauren Johnson, and designer Jane Dixon Smith.

JOIN ALLI

Alliance of Independent Authors

ALLi, the Alliance of Independent Authors is the global association for
self-publishing indie authors.

Join us for reliable advice and advocacy,
discounts, free guidebooks and resources, member forums, contract
review, motivation, education and support from a wonderful indie
author community.

AllianceIndependentAuthors.org

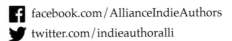

facebook.com/AllianceIndieAuthors
twitter.com/indieauthoralli

MORE ADVICE & FEEDBACK

ADVICE UPDATES FROM ALLI

WOULD YOU LIKE TO RECEIVE A WEEKLY ROUNDUP
OF SELF-PUBLISHING ADVICE
FROM OUR AWARD-WINNING BLOG?

WRITE MORE BOOKS. REACH MORE READERS. SELL MORE BOOKS.
SIGN UP FOR ALLI UPDATES

DIRECT TO YOUR INBOX EACH WEDNESDAY

CREATIVE BUSINESS PLANNING MEMBERSHIP & WORKSHOPS

ALLI DIRECTOR ORNA ROSS RUNS A MONTHLY PAID MEMBERSHIP PROGRAM OFFERING SMALL-GROUP WORKSHOPS, DOWNLOADABLE PLANNERS, FACEBOOK ACCOUNTABILITY GROUP AND OTHER RESOURCES.

THIS IS A PAID PROGRAM THROUGH PATREON AND PLACES ARE LIMITED. FIND OUT MORE.

WE'D LOVE YOUR FEEDBACK
REVIEW REQUEST

I f you enjoyed this book, would you consider leaving a brief review online on your favorite online bookstore that takes reviews: Amazon, Apple, Barnes and Noble Goodreads or Kobo?

A good review is very important to authors these days as it helps other readers know this is a book worth their time.

It doesn't have to be long or detailed. Just a sentence saying what you enjoyed and a star-rating is all that's needed. Many thanks.

PRIZES FOR INDIE AUTHORS
COPYRIGHT © ALLIANCE OF INDEPENDENT AUTHORS 2021

EBOOK: 978-1-913588-31-1
PAPERBACK: 978-1-913588-32-8
LARGE PRINT: 978-1-913588-33-5
HARDBACK: 978-1-913588-34-2
AUDIO: 978-1-913588-35-9

Orna Ross
Publications

Milton Keynes UK
Ingram Content Group UK Ltd.
UKHW051100060224
437337UK00006BA/280